CONTENTS

INTRODUCTION

Confidence comes from feeling good about yourself and believing in your abilities. It's a state of mind which is conveyed to others through your voice, body language, demeanour and actions. Lack of self-confidence is characterised by critical self-talk and self-doubt, which can hold you back and prevent you from realising your full potential. It's important to note that while confident people may doubt themselves from time to time, they don't let their fears stop them from achieving their goals. What many people don't realise is that confidence grows with use, like a muscle. Confident thinking and behaviour can be practised and, in time, it can become a habit. These easy-to-follow tips will help you to understand what affects confidence and how you can build your confidence and self-esteem to a healthy level.

UNDERSTANDING
CONFIDENCE

The first step to improving your self-confidence is to understand how lack of confidence affects you and which situations in particular cause you to feel this way. It's very rare for someone to be unconfident in every area of their life. While you may lack confidence at work or among large groups of people, you may be self-assured in other areas such as cooking, playing sport or dealing with finances.

KEEP A
CONFIDENCE
DIARY

NOTE

In order to understand your confidence issues, take some time to work out what your triggers are, and when your confidence is at its highest or lowest points. Choose a notebook that reflects your personality – be it a simple notepad or an illustrated diary – as you are more likely to want to pick up and use something you like the look of. Keep it where you are most likely to use it: by the bed, in the kitchen, wherever you think you will notice it; but if you are concerned about a loved one delving into your notes, it could be kept in a drawer or cupboard. The act of writing down how you feel and what your confidence levels are like from day to day will not only help you to keep track of what may cause a bout of low confidence, but it will also be cathartic. Remember to write down the high points as well as the lows; the diary will give you something to refer back to on low-confidence days, reminding you that things can be better.

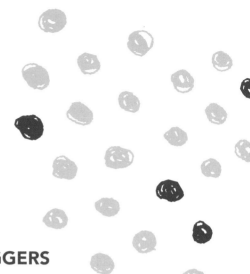

KNOW YOUR TRIGGERS

Once you have been keeping
your diary for a while, you are
likely to start noticing some
patterns. It may be that there
are certain situations that
always knock your confidence,
or that talking to a certain
friend always gives you a boost.
The people and situations
that cause your confidence
levels to drop are known as
'triggers', and one of the
simplest things you can do to
help break this cycle of low
confidence is to avoid them.
A friend who makes you feel
bad about yourself is not a
true friend; a class or event
that leaves you feeling low is
not having a positive effect
on your life. If you cannot
completely avoid your triggers,
then use the tips that follow
as a means to cope with them
and to gradually change them.

BE TRUE TO YOURSELF

An important question to ask yourself is, where do you feel most and least confident? This is not just a question of location – although for some people certain places bolster their confidence or make them feel worse – it is more about the areas of your life you feel are at polar opposites where your confidence is concerned. Someone may, for example, feel that they have raised their family well and be confident as a parent, while lacking in confidence when it comes to work. Knowing the areas, both physical and emotional, which affect your confidence can help you to build your confidence levels. At first, situations or places that knock your confidence can be avoided when your confidence is already at a low point, and later you can work on altering the way you perceive and feel about these situations using the tips in this book, particularly those that emphasise mindfulness.

The POWER of your MIND

Your thoughts affect the way you feel and behave. The habit of thinking negatively about yourself can lead to low self-confidence and self-worth. However, you don't have to be at the mercy of your thinking. The tips in this section reveal how you can take back control by challenging your thoughts to build a more positive self-image.

When starting out on a journey of self-improvement, it can be hard to see what the end result will be. It is easy to become bogged down in the 'what ifs' a situation brings to mind, and this is where visualisation can help. Sitting in a comfortable chair, in a relaxed position, close your eyes and begin to focus on your breathing. There is no need to breathe more slowly, just pay attention to your natural breathing patterns. Next, start to build a picture in your head of how a more confident you would look and act. Where are you? Who is with you? Notice the details and enjoy the feeling of confidence from within. While you are working on building your confidence, take this mental image with you and see it as something to aspire to.

Visualise a more confident you

Try to be like the turtle –
at ease in your own shell.

Bill Copeland

TENSION IS WHO YOU THINK YOU SHOULD BE.

RELAXATION IS WHO YOU ARE.

Chinese proverb

Change Your Thoughts

& You Change Your World

Norman Vincent Peale

Spring-clean your
belief system.
What you believe is
what you become.

Ask yourself 'why?'

One of the key ways to challenge negative thoughts that drain your confidence is to ask 'why?' For example, the commonly held negative thought 'I'm not good enough' can make you worried about many aspects of your life; perhaps you feel you are not good enough at your job, not a good enough friend, not a good enough partner. Now is the time to ask yourself why that is: can you find five empirical reasons why you are not good enough? It is unlikely you can. Let logic prevail; if the only way you can answer this simple question is with 'because I know it's true' or with minor incidents from the past, you can begin to change your self-perception.

WOULD YOU SAY IT TO A FRIEND?

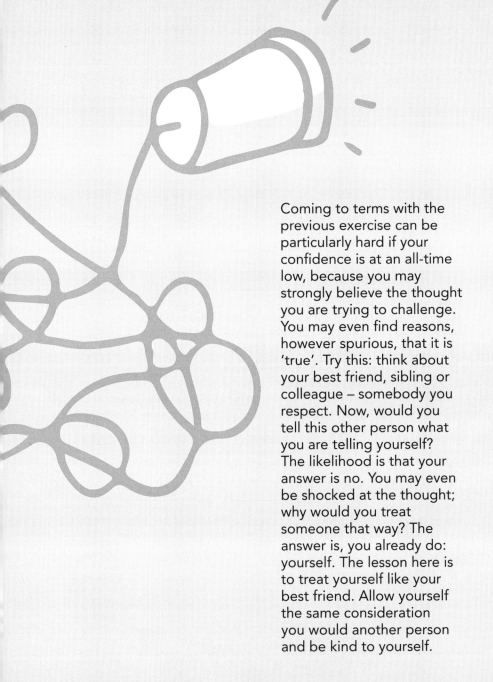

Coming to terms with the previous exercise can be particularly hard if your confidence is at an all-time low, because you may strongly believe the thought you are trying to challenge. You may even find reasons, however spurious, that it is 'true'. Try this: think about your best friend, sibling or colleague – somebody you respect. Now, would you tell this other person what you are telling yourself? The likelihood is that your answer is no. You may even be shocked at the thought; why would you treat someone that way? The answer is, you already do: yourself. The lesson here is to treat yourself like your best friend. Allow yourself the same consideration you would another person and be kind to yourself.

USE MANTRAS

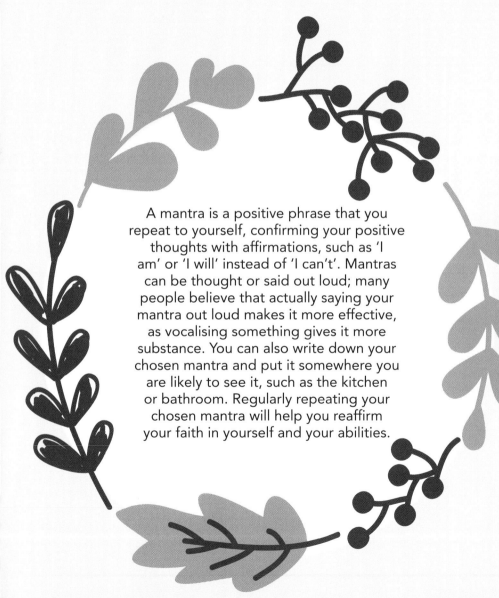

A mantra is a positive phrase that you repeat to yourself, confirming your positive thoughts with affirmations, such as 'I am' or 'I will' instead of 'I can't'. Mantras can be thought or said out loud; many people believe that actually saying your mantra out loud makes it more effective, as vocalising something gives it more substance. You can also write down your chosen mantra and put it somewhere you are likely to see it, such as the kitchen or bathroom. Regularly repeating your chosen mantra will help you reaffirm your faith in yourself and your abilities.

IT IS BEST
TO ACT WITH

Confidence,

NO MATTER HOW LITTLE
RIGHT YOU HAVE TO IT.

Lillian Hellman

MAKE A HAPPY LIST

In order to focus on the positive, try making a list of all the good things in your life. This might seem difficult at first, but you can always ask friends and family for help. The list could be made up of personal or general points, for example 'I am healthy', or 'My family is supportive'. This is something you can pin in a prominent place to remind you of the good around you when negativity seems to be creeping in.

No Need

Perfectionism – the desire to do better
– can be a positive thing. But continually
striving for a perceived version of perfection
can stop you from being happy with who
you already are and from seeing all the
positive things you already achieve. One of
the most common perfectionist tendencies
is to compare yourself with others. This may
take the form of direct comparison, such as
'Thomas is more successful in his job than
I am' or of general comparison along the

to Compare

lines of 'I wish I could be more like Eve'.
Either way, in seeing others as somehow
better than you, you are moving your focus
away from your own positives. In trying
to be like other people, you stop yourself
from being the best version of you. Try
instead to think about what areas of your
life you would like to improve, and work on
those areas without comparing with others,
while recognising your strong points.

WORRY PRETENDS TO BE
NECESSARY BUT SERVES
NO USEFUL PURPOSE.

Eckhart Tolle

IF YOU FOCUS ON LIFE'S POSITIVES, THE NEGATIVES WILL FADE AWAY.

LIST TEN THINGS YOU LIKE ABOUT YOURSELF

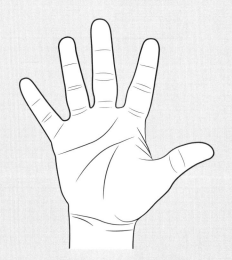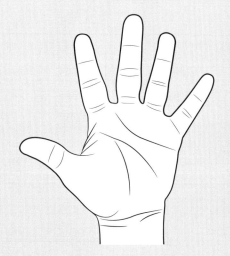

Write down ten things you like about yourself. It doesn't matter how small or 'silly' these things are. Maybe you make the best cup of tea, or you have a talent for making your friends laugh. Focusing on things that you like about yourself will help you to break the habit of putting yourself down. Keep adding to the list and feel your confidence soar.

BODY CONFIDENCE

How you hold your body
affects your state of mind.
This is because your muscles
are directly connected to your
brain's emotional centres. Simple
changes to your posture and
movement can help you to feel
more powerful and in control.

STRAIGHTEN UP

Are you slumping in your chair or slouching your shoulders when you stand? If so, straighten up! Improving your posture can instantly make you appear more positive and confident to others. Research shows it also leads to more confident thoughts and a better mood. Open your chest and keep your head level, and you'll look and feel more assured and poised.

POWER POSE

Two minutes standing in a 'power pose'
can dramatically alter your brain chemistry.
Try adopting a wide stance with your
hands up in the air, as if you've just won
the lottery or your football team has
just scored a goal. Alternatively, try the
'Wonder Woman' pose, with your feet
slightly apart and your hands on your hips.
While you might not want to do this in
the office, you can quickly do this in the
toilets or when no one's about whenever
you need an instant confidence boost.

NOD YOUR HEAD

Nodding your head not only signals 'yes' to other people, it also signals 'yes' to your brain. Researchers think nodding acts as a kind of self-validation, telling yourself that you have confidence in your own thoughts. The important thing to note is that this works whether the thought is positive or negative. If you nod your head while thinking negative thoughts, this can strengthen your disapproval. Nod away whenever you think positive thoughts and you'll give your confidence an extra boost.

WHATEVER
WE
EXPECT
WITH

CONFIDENCE

BECOMES
OUR
OWN

SELF-
FULFILLING

PROPHECY.

Brian Tracy

Act Confident

Acting confidently can make you *feel* more confident. Even if you're feeling anxious, there are clever ways of making yourself appear more confident to others. The following tips will help you to adopt the qualities of a calm, self-assured person.

Say it like you mean it

The tone of voice you adopt when speaking to people will show whether you feel confident or not. If you speak in a way which makes it obvious to the listener that you are nervous, such as in a high-pitched, broken tone, or by speaking too quickly or quietly, they will most likely not take you very seriously. Adopting a deeper, slower, more even tone of voice shows that you feel calm and self-assured, and that you know what you are talking about. This is particularly useful when speaking in public: for example when giving a presentation at work.

MAKE EYE CONTACT

People who make firm eye contact are seen as being more trustworthy and confident. However, connecting with someone's gaze can feel uncomfortable if you are shy or feeling nervous. If you struggle to look people in the eye, try fixing your gaze between the other person's eyes instead. They won't be able to tell you're not looking them directly in the eyes and you'll give the impression of being self-assured and likeable. Just make sure you avert your gaze briefly every seven to ten seconds or so in order to avoid giving them an intimidating stare!

MODEL SOMEONE

One way to improve self-confidence is to model the habits of highly confident people. Find a role model who is confident in the area you would like more confidence – whether that's giving a presentation at work or going on dates – and model as many of their behaviours, attitudes and habits as possible. If you have the chance to talk to them, ask them about their attitude and thought processes. If the person is a well-known figure, you can learn from them by reading their books or biographies, and studying their TV shows, films and interviews.

WITH CONFIDENCE, YOU HAVE WON BEFORE YOU HAVE STARTED.

Marcus Garvey

ACT AS IF YOU HAVE
AMPLE CONFIDENCE

Vividly imagine how your life would be if you were naturally confident right now. How would your posture be? How would you move? How would your voice sound? What would you say to yourself? What would you picture in your mind? Once you have a clear image, imagine you are this person. Step into their shoes and see the world through their eyes; feel what they feel. If you do this often, you'll forget that you're acting and confidence will become a habit.

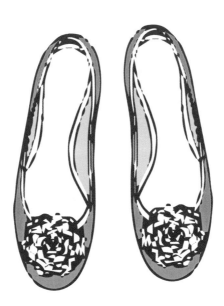

First say to yourself what you would be;

and then do what you have to do.

Epictetus

why not live a

life?

BE ASSERTIVE

When we lack confidence, it can seem like the easier option to bow to the wishes of others and say 'yes' to everything, even if you are really not happy with the situation. Though it seems like the simplest option, doing this in fact negatively affects your confidence, as you are essentially telling yourself that the wishes of others are more important than your own. Being assertive doesn't have to mean being aggressive. The main thing is that you realise your own needs are as important as everybody else's.

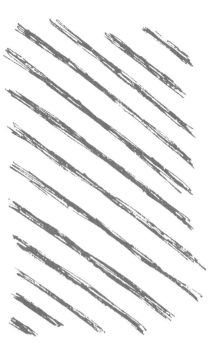

Your boss asks you to take on a new project when you are already overworked and you know that you will not be able to finish it to the necessary standard. Instead of taking it on because you think it is the correct thing to do, explain the situation to your boss, so that a solution can be found.

Your friend asks you to go out, saying you will enjoy it. You know that what you really want today is to stay at home and watch a film. Instead of going out to please your friend, talk to them and let them know that you are not in the mood, and that you will see them soon for another event. The likelihood is that they will appreciate your honesty.

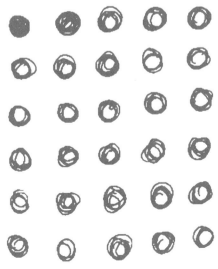

47

WEAR YOUR FAVOURITE
AFTERSHAVE OR PERFUME

Perfume not only makes you smell nice, but it has been proven to boost your confidence, too. When you smell good, you feel good about yourself and feel more attractive. Find a scent that suits your personality; something that makes you feel good the instant you spritz it on. Choose from four fragrance groups – floral and fruity, fresh and zesty, woody and musky, and spicy and oriental. Consider layering your scent by using soap, shower gels and body lotions with similar or complementary scents.

Dream lofty dreams,
and as you dream,
so you shall become.

James Allen

REMAIN *Calm* IN EVERY SITUATION BECAUSE *Peace* EQUALS POWER.

Joyce Meyer

GET SUPERSTITIOUS

Do you have a lucky charm such as a special piece of jewellery or a 'lucky' top? If you do, put it to good use. Research shows indulging in superstitions can improve our performance and chances of success – not because they attract more luck, but because they make us feel more confident. Even good-luck gestures such as crossing your fingers can boost your performance in an exam or sporting event.

Optimism is the faith that leads to achievement.

Nothing can be done without hope and confidence.

Helen Keller

Make *Plans*

and Achieve your Goals

Keeping on top of all there is to do at work and home can feel overwhelming. Take back control by planning and staying organised. Setting goals and working towards them brings a sense of achievement, which can do wonders for your self-esteem.

BE PREPARED FOR
THE DAY AHEAD

The pressure of deadlines, meetings,
phone calls and long working hours
can all build up and cause us to doubt
our ability to handle things, which can
upset confidence levels. This is likely to
not only get in the way of an enjoyable,
effective working life, but can also
have a negative impact on the rest
of your life. A simple way to reduce
this feeling of pressure is to plan and
prepare for your working day. Pack
your lunch the night before so that
you are not rushing to put it together
in the morning. Look up bus or train
times in advance to ensure you know
about any delays, and make a list of the
tasks you wish to complete, so when
you get to your place of work your day
is already planned out. Taking these
steps can give you more confidence
in your workload management.

BELIEVE

IN

YOURSELF

START BY DOING WHAT'S

Necessary

THEN DO WHAT'S

Possible

AND SUDDENLY YOU
ARE DOING THE

impossible.

St Francis of Assisi

TRY A TO-DO LIST

Simple as it may sound, if you are unsure about your organisational skills, then a to-do list may well be the best thing to try. It can seem like there is too much to do and too few hours in the day. This may be true, but getting organised will help you to feel confident in your ability to prioritise tasks and get them done on time. A simple notepad will suffice, or you could even invest in an attractive notebook to write your lists in – if you take pleasure in this simple task it will encourage you to continue the habit. The to-do lists can be as simple or as detailed as you like; the main thing is that they work well for you, and that you enjoy ticking off each task as you complete it as an indication of achievement.

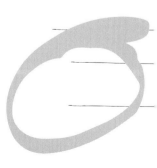

1. Buy milk

2. ...

Big dreams often

have
small
beginnings.

There is no
chance, no
destiny,
no fate,
that can
circumvent
or hinder
or control
the firm
resolve of a
determined
soul.

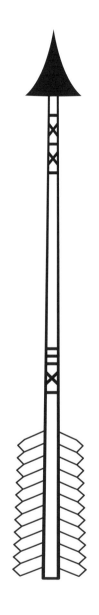

Ella Wheeler Wilcox

GET COMFORTABLE BEING UNCOMFORTABLE

Life can make you feel uncomfortable but this doesn't have to stop you from achieving your goals. In fact, if you can be comfortable with feeling uncomfortable, you'll have the confidence to handle whatever situation comes your way. Unfortunately, most of us avoid discomfort. We live within small, familiar comfort zones which limit what we do in our lives. When you regularly take risks, however, your comfort zone expands. Even taking small steps towards your goals can expand your comfort zone and make you feel more positive about life. Remember, feeling uncomfortable is usually a good sign – it means you're moving forwards and exploring new territory. You're open to new people, places, experiences and adventures in your life!

THERE'S NO SUCH THING AS FAILURE

It is quite possible that, even if you set the most relevant, realistic goals, you may not achieve them in the way or the time you wanted to. Life may throw something unexpected in your path, which stops you from achieving what you want, when you want. This is not failure. Feeling like you have failed is bound to lead to low mood, and can often come about if things haven't quite gone according to plan. However, the best thing to do is to draw a mental line under the experience, learn from what has happened and try again. As long as you are still trying, you are working towards your long-term aims; and as long as you are doing that, you are never truly failing.

Whatever has happened in the past, you can always take a fresh step into a future full of new hopes.

Your brain and body can't tell the difference between something you vividly imagine and something that's real. That's why your mouth waters when you imagine biting into a slice of chocolate cake. You can use this to your advantage if you're feeling nervous about doing something for the first time, such as giving a speech. By closing your eyes and repeatedly imagining yourself wildly succeeding, you create neural pathways in your brain which programme you to perform well the next time you give a speech in real life. In order for this to be effective, you need to run your mental movie repeatedly and you need to engage all your senses, so that the movie is as vivid and realistic as possible. Picture your surroundings, hear the sound of your voice, see the audience respond enthusiastically and feel the excitement and confidence inside you.

Treat Yourself Well,

With our hectic lives, it can be easy to forget to be loving and kind to ourselves. Treating yourself as well as you would treat a best friend will give you an inner and outer glow.

Feel Well

MAKE
bath time
SACRED

A soak in the bath can do wonders.
As well as keeping you clean and
fresh, a warm bath with your
favourite bubbles or oils helps relax
tense muscles and prepares the
body for sleep – and being well
rested boosts confidence levels.
Make the most of your bath;
invest in some bath products that
make you feel good, light some
candles and maybe take a book
with you to read while you soak.

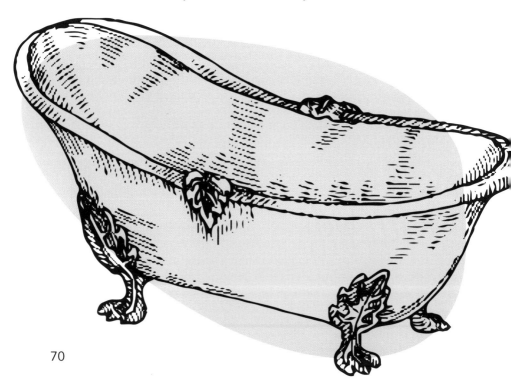

Take the time to let yourself really relax into the water and use your favourite body wash to cleanse away the day. This treat will make you feel more in tune with yourself, and help you feel better both physically and emotionally. If you don't have a bathtub, or if it's a particularly hot day, a luxurious shower can give you the same benefits. The water on your skin can invigorate and refresh, and washing with your favourite shower gel or scrub, enjoying the scent of it on your skin, can give your confidence a real boost.

It can be hard to find motivation when you're feeling sleep deprived, and many aspects of our lives can fall by the wayside, leading to lack of confidence in our abilities. Being well rested makes us feel calmer, more confident and improves concentration, so why not give your bedtime routine a shake-up and see what good comes of it?

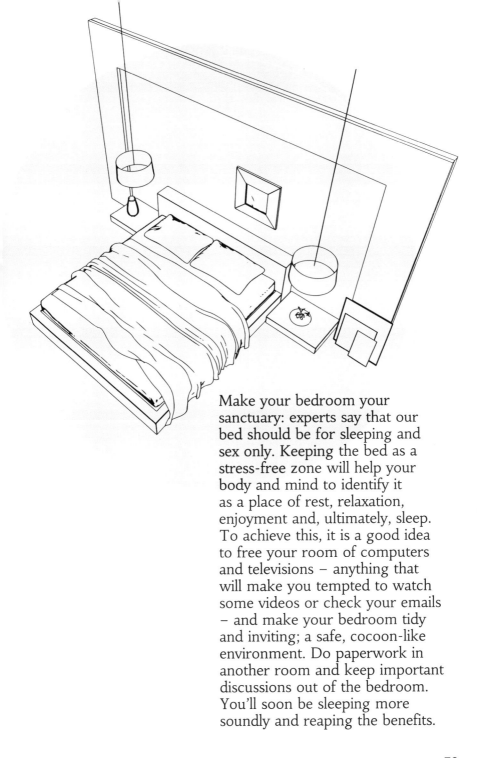

Make your bedroom your sanctuary: experts say that our bed should be for sleeping and sex only. Keeping the bed as a stress-free zone will help your body and mind to identify it as a place of rest, relaxation, enjoyment and, ultimately, sleep. To achieve this, it is a good idea to free your room of computers and televisions – anything that will make you tempted to watch some videos or check your emails – and make your bedroom tidy and inviting; a safe, cocoon-like environment. Do paperwork in another room and keep important discussions out of the bedroom. You'll soon be sleeping more soundly and reaping the benefits.

BE THE CALM CENTRE IN THE RAGING FLOW OF LIFE.

Leo Babauta

PROGRESSIVE
RELAXATION

Just like meditation and yoga, progressive relaxation is an excellent sleep aid. It is often the case that when low mood strikes and our confidence has dipped, we lie awake at night unable to relax. The following exercise removes the pressure, breaking relaxation down into smaller steps. Start at your feet and work your way up your body, concentrating on one body part at a time. For each body part, clench it as tightly as you can before letting it go, feeling the physical relaxation that comes with this release. Some people find it helpful to use a verbal aid, for example by saying or thinking, 'I am relaxing my feet; my feet are now completely relaxed', and repeating for each body part.

Invest in some 'me' time

It is all too easy to believe that all your time should be spent doing 'useful' things, or being there for other people. This is not always true, and trying to keep going all the time for the sake of others, without giving yourself the space to just enjoy your own company, will leave you feeling drained and tired – allowing negativity to creep in. For a positivity boost, try taking the night off. Indulge in your favourite foods, watch a film or series that you love, pick up a book you've been meaning to read and, most importantly, switch off from the rest of the world. Perhaps you want to pamper yourself, too, giving your feet a soak or indulging in an extra-long bath. You will likely feel all the more positive for giving your batteries a chance to recharge.

Always be a

first-rate

version · of · yourself,

instead of

a second-rate version

· of · someone else.

Judy Garland

Cherish compliments

Receiving genuine, heartfelt compliments can boost our self-esteem – so don't brush them off. Thank the person who has complimented you and take a moment to truly internalise what has just been said. In the same way, savour any words of praise from family, friends and work colleagues. Save complimentary emails, cards and messages, and file away your best performance reviews at work. Read these words of praise whenever you need a quick shot of confidence.

One positive thought in the morning can change your whole day.

I have two
bowls of
confidence
for
breakfast
each
morning.

Eric Bristow

Mix with positive people

Happy, smiling faces are infectious! Spending time with positive, supportive people will rub off on you and put you in a positive frame of mind. Friends can build you up and improve your self-confidence and self-worth. Friends support our efforts to achieve our goals – they celebrate our successes and wipe away our tears when things don't go according to plan. They can be a sounding board for ideas and provide a valuable second opinion. Sadly, not all friends are supportive; if the people you mix with tend to drain you or bring you down a lot, it's probably time to get some new friends!

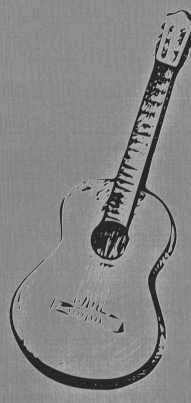

Learn something new

Whether it's taking driving lessons, learning a new language or discovering a new hobby, mastering something new can lead to increased self-esteem. Admittedly, it takes courage to be a beginner again and acquire new skills, but the satisfaction of venturing out of our comfort zones and doing something well can make us feel good about ourselves. Is there an instrument you have always wanted to play or a sport you fancy trying? Or you might prefer to learn something practical like baking or gardening. Research shows that people who continue to learn throughout their lives are more optimistic and have a higher sense of self-worth. Plus, if you attend a class, meeting people there is a great way to enhance your social life.

The most Beautiful thing you can wear is Confidence.

Blake Lively

Look Good, Feel Great

Feeling good about your appearance goes more than skin deep. Feeling happy with what you see in the mirror each day can help you to feel more relaxed and self-assured, which will have a knock-on effect on your mood and confidence.

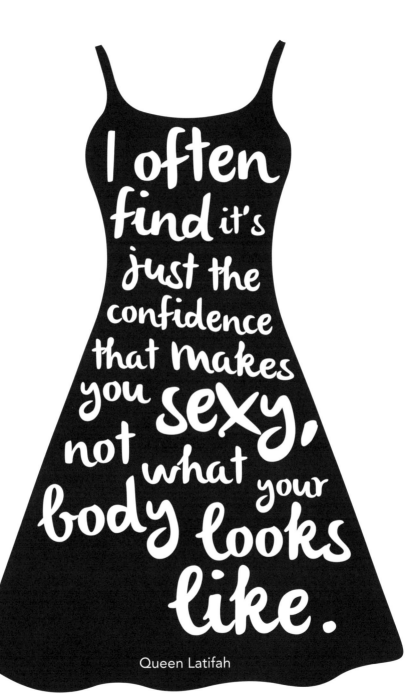

I often find it's just the confidence that makes you sexy, not what your body looks like.

Queen Latifah

Have a good hair day

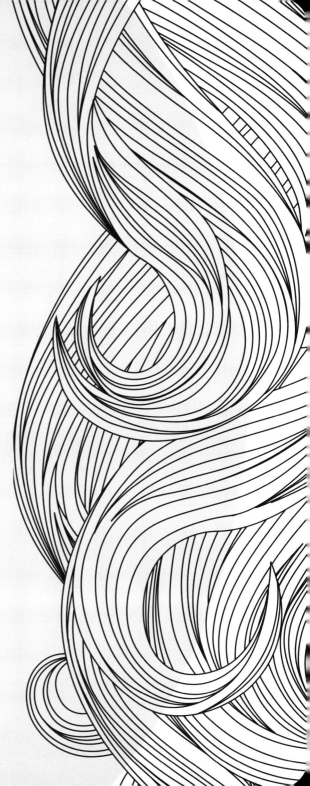

Looking after your hair is an excellent way to improve the way you feel about your body. Make sure you wash and condition as often as you need to, with products designed for your hair type: for example, dry, oily, coloured or curly hair each need different types of care. If you feel in need of a bigger boost, why not invest in a hair masque to pamper yourself with, or try out a new haircut or colour to show the new, more positive you. Be daring and show your personal style, and feel your positive energy building.

BE
THE BEST
VERSION
OF
YOU

Dress to impress

Does your current wardrobe leave something to be desired? Now might be the time to replenish it with clothes which flatter you and make you feel good. The way you dress affects the way you feel, from the colours you choose to how an item fits. The old adage says, 'dress for the job you want, not the one you have'. Choose clothes that fit well and reflect your personality. Make sure that when you look in the mirror, what you are wearing makes you think 'yes, I look good today', rather than 'what am I wearing?' or 'it will have to do'. Feeling good in your clothes will make you feel more comfortable in yourself, and boost your confidence levels both in the workplace and socially.

Style is whatever you want to do, if you can do it with confidence.

George Clinton

Clear out your wardrobe

Wearing clothes that don't fit well, or you feel uncomfortable in, can make you want to fade into the background, so try getting rid of your oldest clothes, or the ones that you feel just don't suit you any more. Decluttering has a calming effect which can help stress levels and leave your emotions more balanced. Make sure that the clothes you keep are the ones you really feel good in, and which make the most of your body shape. Your old ones don't have to go to landfill either; try selling them on sites like eBay, or taking them to your local charity shop or clothes bank where you will have the extra self-esteem boost of knowing your unwanted items have helped a charitable cause.

New for old

Once you've had your clear-out, and have your basic wardrobe down to the things you really feel good in, it's time to replace the old with something fresh. Revamping your wardrobe has multiple benefits for your self-esteem; you will most likely feel better about the way you look, and you'll be able to make the best of your body shape, whatever that may be. Choose new clothes that reflect your personality as well as being suitable for your lifestyle and career. Remember, new to you doesn't have to mean brand new. Setting yourself up with a wardrobe to be proud of can be done on a shoestring and can be great fun. Try hunting for bargains at your local charity shops, car-boot sales, and on websites such as eBay and Preloved.

Colour me happy

As well as choosing the right styles and cuts, your new wardrobe should be full of colours that suit your skin tone and boost your mood. Yellow is said to make you feel happier, blue is meant to calm and red is a power colour. If you are a fan of monochrome, you can still add these extra colours with accessories, such as a brightly coloured scarf, or with make-up, if you wear it.

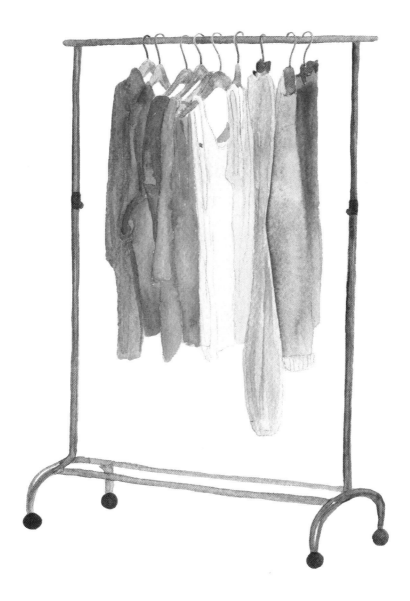

YOU WERE BORN TO BE

REAL,

NOT

Perfect

be brave. take risks.

NOTHING CAN SUBSTITUTE

experience.

Paulo Coelho

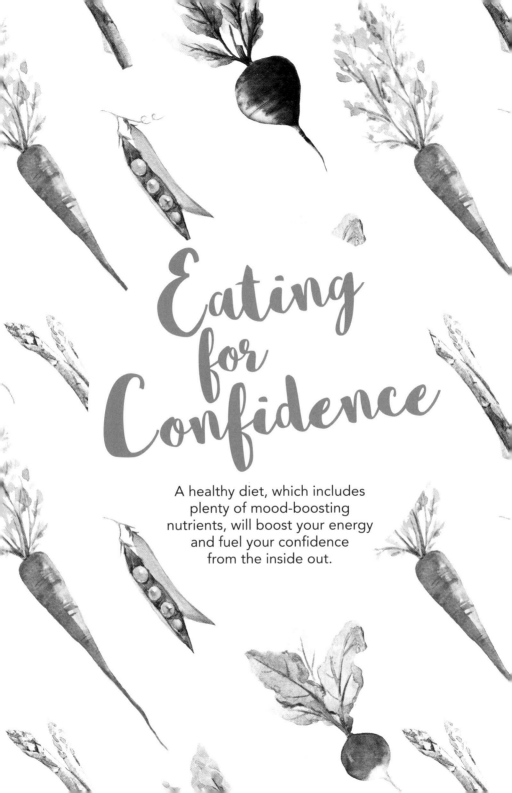

Eating
for
Confidence

A healthy diet, which includes
plenty of mood-boosting
nutrients, will boost your energy
and fuel your confidence
from the inside out.

EAT A BALANCED DIET

Before we look at the specific nutrients that can be beneficial to confidence, it is important to ensure you have a balanced diet. Eating the right amount of calories for your age, height and sex, and ensuring you get enough protein, fibre and vitamin-rich fruit and vegetables, while avoiding too many refined foods, will give you a good basis for general health and well-being. It should also improve digestion, which will make you feel healthier overall.

STAY HYDRATED

As well as being essential for good health, staying hydrated is good for your self-esteem as it helps your skin and hair look their best, which helps boost body confidence. Water also helps to flush out your system, keeping your bowels in working order and reducing feelings of bloating or puffiness. Drinking two litres of water each day is generally recommended for optimum health.

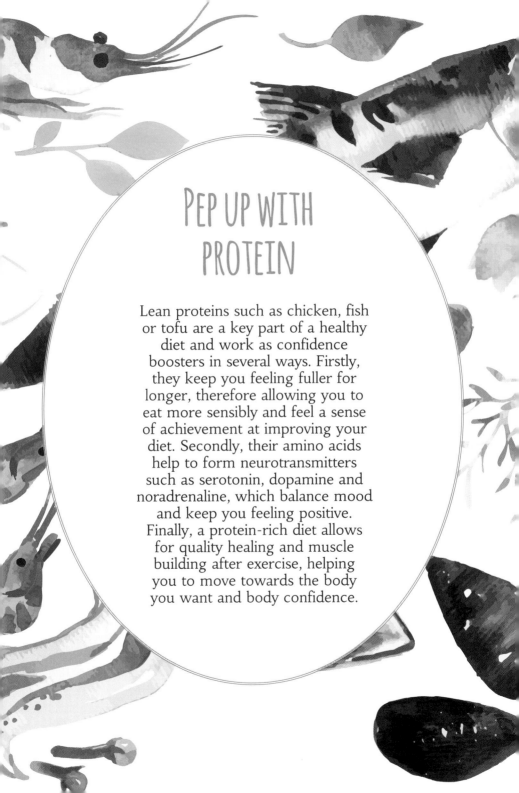

Pep up with PROTEIN

Lean proteins such as chicken, fish or tofu are a key part of a healthy diet and work as confidence boosters in several ways. Firstly, they keep you feeling fuller for longer, therefore allowing you to eat more sensibly and feel a sense of achievement at improving your diet. Secondly, their amino acids help to form neurotransmitters such as serotonin, dopamine and noradrenaline, which balance mood and keep you feeling positive. Finally, a protein-rich diet allows for quality healing and muscle building after exercise, helping you to move towards the body you want and body confidence.

the BEST is yet to come.

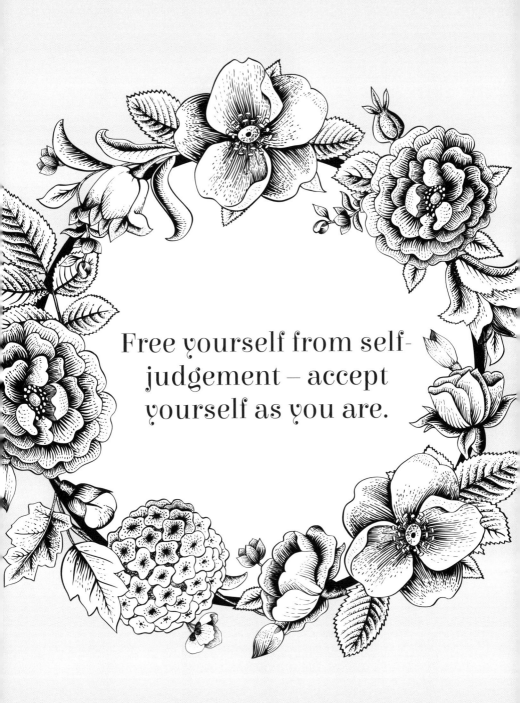

Free yourself from self-judgement – accept yourself as you are.

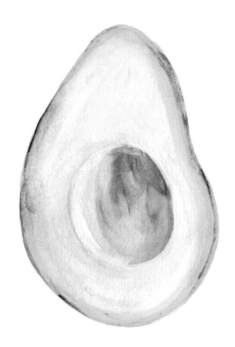

Learn about

When trying to eat healthily, it can be easy to see fat as the enemy. Many 'healthy' products are marketed as low-fat or fat-free, and we are led to believe that fat makes you fat. This is not entirely true. Fats are an important part of your diet. They are key in neurotransmitter production due to the amino acids they

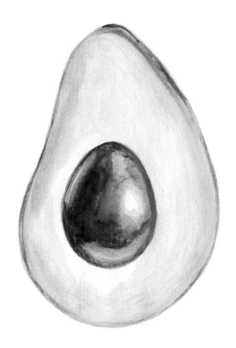

GOOD FATS

contain, and unsaturated fats are
important for healthy skin and
hair, which in turn will make
you feel more confident about
yourself. As long as you get the
balance right, and are eating
plenty of monounsaturated
and polyunsaturated fats, such
as those found in avocados,
olive oil and seeds, you will
start to feel the benefits.

Cut down on caffeine

Caffeine and other similar stimulants should be avoided as much as possible. Many of us rely on that first cup of coffee in the morning to wake us up, or a cup of tea to keep us going at midday, but these caffeinated drinks – along with cola and foods containing caffeine, such as chocolate – could be having an adverse effect on your confidence by increasing your stress levels. Having a caffeinated drink can make us feel more alert because it induces the initial stages of the stress reaction, boosting cortisol

production. Consuming large quantities of caffeine, however, can cause the exhaustion phase of stress and lead to anxiety, which can have a very negative impact on confidence levels. Added to this, caffeine can be very addictive and stopping suddenly can cause withdrawal symptoms, which can make you feel physically unwell and emotionally under pressure – not a good combination for confidence. Try cutting down slowly to no more than 300 mg of caffeine a day; that's the equivalent of three mugs of coffee or four mugs of tea. Have fun experimenting with the huge variety of herbal teas and decaffeinated coffees and teas available on the market (ginseng, ginger and lemon teas are all great for boosting energy), and notice the improvement in your mood and ability to cope.

BE NATURALLY SWEET

Low self-esteem can lead us to make poor food choices as we try to find comfort from food; sweet foods such as cake and chocolate offer the short-term surge of energy you may crave. Snacking on sugar-rich foods can have a very negative effect on the body both physically and emotionally; the inevitable weight gain can make you feel unhappy with your body, and has the potential to make you feel you have 'given in' to certain foods. This can be a cause of stress, which in turn can lead us to reach for sugary foods again, forming a vicious cycle. Our modern lifestyles, however, mean that our stress is more likely to be because of bills we have to pay, or meetings we have to arrange, and reaching for the sugar is unhelpful because we do not really need the energy boost. Try satisfying your sweet tooth by eating naturally sweet foods such as berries, sweet potatoes, carrots and coconut.

Aim for the moon. If you miss, you may hit a star.

W. Clement Stone

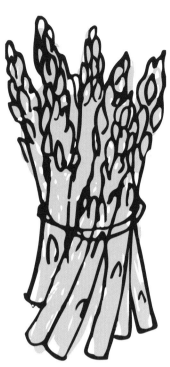

GET A BOOST WITH B VITAMINS

The B-vitamin group is particularly important for maintaining a balanced mood. Among their other functions, B vitamins are involved in the body's control of tryptophan, a building block for serotonin. Vitamin B6 is essential in the production of GABA (gamma-aminobutyric acid), which helps boost mood in a similar way to serotonin. A lack of these essential neurotransmitters can lead to low mood, which in turn can lead to very serious psychological problems. The main vitamins to pay attention to are B1, B3, B5, B6, B9 and B12, all of which can be found in a balanced diet. If you eat a lot of processed foods, or follow a vegan diet, you may be lacking in certain B vitamins, in which case adding a B-vitamin supplement to your diet can have an excellent effect on your overall health and mood.

CALM DOWN WITH CALCIUM

Calcium has a soothing, calming effect and is important in maintaining a balanced mood. It is best consumed alongside vitamin D, which also helps to enhance mood. Calcium is found in dairy foods such as milk, as well as in green leafy vegetables like kale and broccoli, lentils, beans, Brazil nuts and a wide variety of other vegetables. Fortified breakfast cereals and soya alternatives to dairy also provide a good source of calcium, and it is even found in tap water, especially in hard-water areas.

ONCE A
BELIEF
BECOMES
A DEEP
CONVICTION,
THINGS
BEGIN TO
HAPPEN.

WATCH YOUR ALCOHOL INTAKE

When feeling low, for example after a hard day at work, or when lacking confidence in a social situation, many people will reach for a drink to help them relax. Alcohol does have an instantly calming effect, but this is negated by the depressant qualities of alcohol, and the feeling of anxiety that can be left behind once the effects wear off. Alcohol can also disturb your sleep, contrary to the popular idea of a 'nightcap'. Try to cut down your drinking as much as possible, and if you do go for a tipple, opt for a small glass of Chianti, Merlot or Cabernet Sauvignon, as the plant chemicals called procyanidins which are abundant in these particular wines are beneficial to health, especially cardiovascular health. These wines are also rich in melatonin, the sleep hormone, and a well-rested person is more likely to be a confident person.

YOUR HEART KNOWS. LISTEN TO YOUR HEART.

116

EXERCISING YOUR WAY TO CONFIDENCE

Exercise is an important tool for building confidence. As well as toning your muscles, regular exercise will reduce stress and help you to feel more comfortable in your own skin. Whether you join a gym or walk in a park, moving your body will give you a sense of accomplishment and a more positive body image.

WALK TALL

Starting to exercise can be daunting, especially if your confidence is already rather low. Joining a gym or going to a class can seem like the last thing you would want to do. However, exercise can be as simple as going for a walk. Just a 30-minute walk each day can significantly improve your health and emotional well-being. You can fit this in on the way to work, at lunchtime or whenever feels right for you. The best walks are in daylight, in natural surroundings. Not only will being outdoors offer a natural boost, helping you feel better and lifting your spirits, but the exercise itself will also produce endorphins, making you feel great, and seeing your body shape change and become more toned is bound to give your confidence a lift.

SWIM TOWARDS A MORE CONFIDENT YOU

Swimming is one of the most effective forms of exercise, both in terms of giving you a full body workout and in allowing you to relax and unwind. The rhythmic lap of the water with each stroke, and the focus on your technique and breathing, really make this a great way to move your mind away from your worries, allowing some quality time to yourself. This alone time can give you a chance to reflect on the positive changes you are making. Add to that the fact that floating in water is a wonderfully soothing experience, and all part and parcel of a trip to the pool, and you've got a perfect recipe for confidence-boosting relaxation.

INACTION BREEDS
DOUBT AND FEAR.

*Action breeds
confidence
and courage.*

Dale Carnegie

SO THE PIE ISN'T PERFECT?

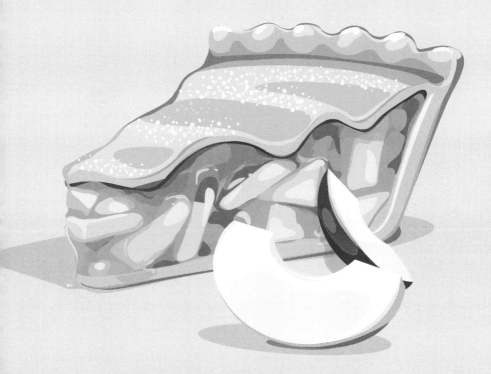

CUT IT INTO WEDGES.
STAY IN CONTROL
AND NEVER PANIC.

Martha Stewart

GET INTO
GARDENING

As well as being a great way to burn calories, being in the garden is a form of 'green exercise' – activity that takes place in nature – which research shows has even more health and well-being benefits than, say, visits to the gym. Gardening can improve your mood, ease muscle tension and lower blood pressure. Feeling close to nature can give you the boost you need to keep calm under pressure, and the act of pruning, weeding, planting and seeing something grow gives you something to look forward to and feel proud of, which is sure to raise your confidence levels.

Turn
I CAN'T
into
I CAN.

YOGA FOR INNER AND OUTER STRENGTH

The ancient practice of yoga is not just about bending your body, but also about bringing balance to your mind. Yoga is practised at your own pace, allowing you to take time to really understand what your body can do. It can help with confidence because of the strengthening and toning effect it has on the body, and because of the calming effect it has on the mind. Most classes will finish with yogic sleep, or guided meditation, which can leave you feeling refreshed, happier and more in touch with yourself. If you would rather not attend a class, yoga can be practised at home with the help of books, DVDs or online demonstrations.

Never apologise for being you.

AS IS OUR CONFIDENCE, SO IS OUR CAPACITY.

William Hazlitt

'GREEN' EXERCISE FOR A NATURAL BOOST

'Green' exercise is any physical activity you take part in outside, in natural surroundings. Enjoy what the great outdoors has to offer by spending more time in your garden, local park or woods. Being in natural surroundings can bring a real sense of tranquillity. Exercising outdoors, be it on the coast, through fields or even just in your own garden, can improve your mood, ease muscle tension and lower blood pressure. Feeling close to nature may give you the boost you need to keep calm under pressure, and feel balanced and content.

DANCE YOURSELF
FIT AND HAPPY

Dancing is, for many people, one of the most
fun ways to get fit, and alongside releasing the
mood-boosting endorphins exercise provides,
it's a great positivity cocktail. It can be as
simple as putting on your favourite music at
home and dancing around your living room
or bedroom, or you could try a class. Jive,
jazz, ballroom and Latin dance classes are all
great ways to get fit and meet new people,
and fitness fusion classes such as Zumba
are becoming ever-more popular. Choose a
style that suits you and, above all, enjoy it.

WHEN FACED WITH AN UPHILL STRUGGLE,

WE GAIN STRENGTH, AND COURAGE, AND CONFIDENCE BY EACH EXPERIENCE IN WHICH WE STOP TO LOOK FEAR IN THE FACE.

Eleanor Roosevelt

Relaxing

Daily life can sometimes feel like an endless, exhausting to-do list. If your stress levels are rising and you're feeling overwhelmed, the following stress-busting tips can help. Reducing your anxiety will help you to feel more confident and in control.

Write away your worries

Everyone will have periods of worry at some point – family, finances, career and health can all be sources of anxiety. Not being able to 'switch off' and continuing to worry about several different things at once can make us feel out of control and therefore knock our confidence. Writing these worries down allows you to voice them, helping you to think more clearly and allowing you to relax more easily. Some people find a further step helpful: if you destroy the paper the worries are listed on by, for example, either ripping it up or throwing it into a fire, you can actually see your worries move from your mind, to the paper and then away.

remain *calm, serene,* always in control of *yourself.* You will then find out how easy it is to *get along.*

Paramahansa Yogananda

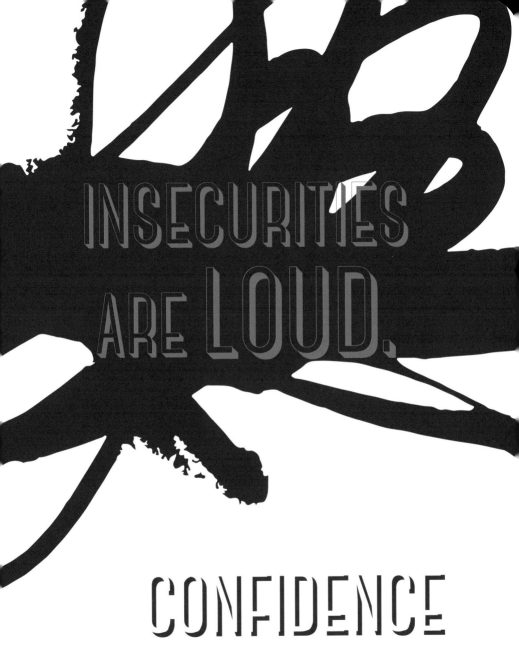

INSECURITIES ARE LOUD.

CONFIDENCE IS SILENT.

Keep it simple

Having too many things going on around you at once can be a major cause of stress, and can give your confidence a knock, particularly if you feel like you cannot get through all the tasks ahead of you. One key example of this is clutter; having too much 'stuff' around you can cause stress as there is always something to think about, something to put away, something to clean (cleaning is harder, too, with so many items to move and clean under or around) etc. Furthermore, this excess of things can make it hard to concentrate on the task at hand, as it causes distractions. Decluttering, throwing out old items that are no longer of use and giving them to a charity shop or using sites such as Freecycle and eBay is a great first step to simplifying your life, leaving you feeling more in control, less stressed, and more confident in your ability to look after yourself and your home.

Talk to a friend or family member

If you think stresses and worries are affecting your confidence, talking to someone close to you can be a huge help. Vocalising your concerns, and hearing the reassurance and advice of someone whose opinions you trust, can alleviate anxiety and let us see that we are not alone. If you do not have someone to confide in, a counsellor or a service such as the Samaritans can provide the sympathetic ear you seek. The simple act of picking up the phone to talk to someone takes faith and demonstrates that you can be a confident, open person.

AVOID 'CATCHING' STRESS FROM YOUR COLLEAGUES

For many, the workplace is the most stressful area of their lives. A large amount of workplace stress is so-called 'second-hand' stress. When a colleague is feeling stressed you can unconsciously absorb their feelings of negativity. To avoid this, if a colleague is talking about work or personal problems, try to say something positive about the subject or offer them some advice. If they carry on, perhaps go to make a hot drink, or, if you cannot walk away, make sure you stay positive and try your best not to adopt your colleague's mindset. It takes faith to challenge a colleague's negativity, so as well as reducing stress, this can boost your confidence by showing you that you are capable of taking up such a challenge.

Financial worries are one of today's biggest stressors, with more and more people in debt and/or out of work. Taking control of your finances is a great confidence boost as it helps reduce the stress that can bring your confidence levels down, and it shows that you can take a situation on and improve it.

Thankfully, there are some simple ways to cut back on non-essential spending. Cancel any direct debits for services you do not want or need; for example, do you have a film club membership or subscriptions you hardly use? Cut it.

Next, look at debt – make sure you are paying off the debts with the highest interest rates first, so as to save money on interest. If you have a lot of credit card debt, now might be the time to take drastic action and cut up your maxed-out credit card – that way you can pay it off and not run up more debt. Finally, it is important that when you do spend your money, it is on the things that are important to you and make you happiest. For example, is your weekly night out with friends high on your list? If so, make sure you put some money aside for it.

A wise man makes his own decisions; an ignorant man follows public opinion.

Chinese proverb

THERE IS NO ONE WHO CAN TELL YOU WHO TO BE...

except yourself.

Treatments and Therapies

Complementary therapies are a great way to give you some more 'me' time and help you to relax. There's a wide range of therapies to choose from. Each should leave you feeling physically and mentally refreshed and ready to tackle the world again.

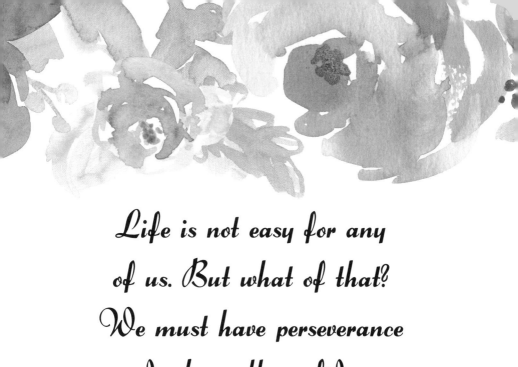

Life is not easy for any
of us. But what of that?
We must have perseverance
and, above all, confidence
in ourselves. We must
believe that we are gifted
for something and that this
thing must be attained.

Marie Curie

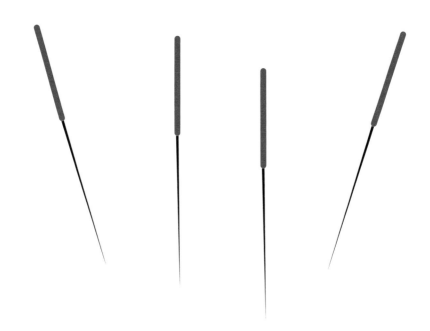

Feel better with acupressure

Acupressure is a part of traditional Chinese medicine and has been practised for many centuries. Similar to acupuncture, but without the use of needles, this gentle therapy involves applying pressure to certain pressure points to promote the free flow of energy or 'qi' through the body. Acupressure is known to help relieve muscle tension and boost circulation, both of which will leave you feeling calmer. You can go to a practitioner for acupressure or use simple acupressure techniques at home. There are many books available on the subject, or you can find tutorials online.

YOU HAVE TO HAVE
CONFIDENCE IN
YOUR ABILITY,

AND THEN BE TOUGH ENOUGH
TO FOLLOW THROUGH.

Rosalynn Carter

TRY EFT

EFT (emotional freedom techniques) use tapping to unlock blocked energy, therefore improving health and well-being. Like acupuncture and acupressure, the techniques are based on the idea of 'qi' or energy moving through 'meridians' in the body, with blockages in these meridians causing illness and emotional problems. With EFT, you hold on to the negative emotion or thought that is blocking you while tapping on the relevant body point, then you do the same again, only this time using a positive statement to replace the negative thought. EFT can easily be tried at home, with online tutorials and illustrations readily available.

Don't take yourself too seriously.

If you **love** what you do, you can achieve *anything.*

Keep your head up and your heart open.

REFLEXOLOGY FOR BALANCE AND CALM

Reflexology is similar to acupressure, using stimulation of certain points to help the flow of energy through the body. These points are found on the feet, hands and face, but practitioners will usually use the feet as these are more sensitive, and are believed to have points which relate to every part of the body. Stimulating these points is meant to release energy blockages in the related body part, therefore facilitating the free flow of energy through that body part, and helping to reduce illness. The relaxation alone can help reduce stress and make you feel more balanced. For practicality, if you decide to try this on yourself, it may be easier to use your hands and, although reflexology can be self-practised, it is more beneficial to visit a trained reflexologist for treatment. Look up your local natural health centre for more information.

Health

IS THE GREATEST

possession.

Contentment

IS THE GREATEST

treasure.

Confidence

IS THE GREATEST

friend.

Lao Tzu

AND FINALLY...
SEEKING
MEDICAL
ADVICE

If your confidence issues are having a negative effect on your day-to-day life, it is worth speaking to your doctor about it. Although complementary therapies can help a great deal, some situations need a firmer hand and sometimes low self-confidence is a sign of more serious issues. It may be that your doctor recommends a talking therapy such as CBT (cognitive behavioural therapy), or medication, to help you get to a better place. Remember, the doctor is there to help you, not to judge; tell them everything and that way they will be able to give you the best possible advice.

WE HOPE YOU ENJOY THE JOURNEY TOWARDS A NEW, MORE CONFIDENT YOU!

Have you enjoyed this book?

If so, why not write a review on your favourite website?

If you're interested in finding out more about our books,
find us on Facebook at Summersdale Publishers
and follow us on Twitter at @Summersdale.

Thanks very much for buying this Summersdale book.

www.summersdale.com